Thomas Edison
INCREDIBLE INVENTOR

Thomas Edison
INCREDIBLE INVENTOR

By Louis Sabin and JoAnn Early Macken

Illustrated by George Ulrich

SCHOLASTIC INC.

New York   Toronto   London   Auckland   Sydney
Mexico City   New Delhi   Hong Kong   Buenos Aires

ISBN-13: 978-0-439-88006-0
ISBN-10: 0-439-88006-8

12 11 10 9 8 7 6 5 4 3   8 9 10 11/0

Printed in the U.S.A.   23
First printing, September 2006

CONTENTS

CHAPTER 1:

A Curious Boy

On a warm spring day, a small, brown-haired boy sat on the ground outside a barn. He enjoyed watching the animals. Chickens, pigs, horses, a couple of cows, and a flock of geese lived on the farm. One of the geese caught the boy's atten-

tion. Young Thomas Alva Edison watched the bird.

The goose sat on three eggs nestled in a pile of straw. Once in a while, she got off the eggs, turned them a little, and sat down again. The boy wanted to know why the goose did that. He waited to see what would happen.

"Peep-peep! Peep-peep!"

The goose moved off the eggs. They didn't look the same anymore. One was cracked in half. A tiny, down-covered head stuck out. Another egg began to crack open.

"A baby goose!" the boy cried out. "That's what the big goose was doing!"

Al—as everyone called him then— thought about the way the egg had hatched for a long time. It was the most exciting thing he had ever seen.

The next morning, Al ran out to the barn without waiting for breakfast. He picked up an armload of straw and shaped it into a nest. Then he went into the henhouse and came out with two eggs. He put them in his nest and carefully sat on them.

Time passed. Al got up and turned his eggs the way the goose had turned her eggs. He sat down again. After a while, his father came into the barn. "What are you doing, Al?" Samuel Edison asked.

"Hatching chickens," the boy answered.

Mr. Edison scratched his head and smiled. "Sorry, son," he said. "I'm afraid it won't work."

"Why not, Papa?" the boy asked.

Mr. Edison explained that only a hen could hatch chicken eggs. She knew just how warm to keep them and just when to

turn each one. It was something people couldn't do. Still, Al's father told himself, it was pretty good thinking for such a young boy—and just like Al to come up with an idea like that!

Al always wanted to know about everything around him. He looked and listened and asked countless questions. If someone didn't know the answer to one of his questions, he asked, "Why don't you know?"

CHAPTER 2:
A New Town

Al wandered freely over the family's land. He climbed down a bluff to the local canal and sometimes even fell in. He explored the town and visited people as they worked. To young Thomas Edison, born on February 11, 1847, in Milan, Ohio, his hometown was a wonderful place.

Milan was a busy town. A canal connected it to Lake Erie. With horses or oxen, farmers from all over the state brought their crops to Milan. Dock workers loaded the crops onto ships that went up the canal

to the lake. From there, the ships traveled to big cities such as Cleveland and Buffalo. Near the canal, workers built more ships.

Milan was also a stopping place for wagon trains heading west. Wagons drove through the town one after another, especially after gold was discovered in California in 1849. Little Al liked to talk to the travelers. He wanted to know where they were coming from, where they were going, and why. He wanted to know everything!

Mr. and Mrs. Edison never stopped Al from doing anything as long as it was safe. Al was the youngest of the Edisons' seven children. The whole family enjoyed the little boy's clever remarks. He had many friends in the neighborhood. Everyone gave him lots of attention.

In 1853, a railroad was built about ten miles away from Milan. It changed the town. Farmers began to ship their crops by train because it was faster and cheaper. They didn't need the canal, and they had no reason to come to Milan. Business slowed down, stores closed, and the canal carried no more ships. The busy little town was busy no more.

The next year, when Al was seven, the Edisons boarded a steamship and moved to a new home near Port Huron, Michigan. There they had a garden, an orchard, and a stable for horses.

Port Huron was a large, booming town right on Lake Huron and only a few miles from Canada. Mr. Edison did well there. He ran a lumber business, sold grain and feed for animals, and grew crops on his land. In the yard, he built an observation tower with a telescope at the top. Visitors

could climb more than one hundred feet to view the landscape. Al spent much of his free time playing up there or just looking out over the land.

Shortly after the move, Al came down with scarlet fever. He was sick for a long time. The illness affected his hearing, and he never heard well again.

CHAPTER 3:
School Days

In Port Huron, Al attended school for about three months. The school was run by the Reverend G. B. Engle and his wife. The students had to learn their lessons by heart and recite them on command. The rest of the time, they were ordered to sit up straight and be quiet. If they made any mistakes in their work, giggled, whispered, or misbehaved, Reverend Engle punished them.

So used to freedom, Al couldn't stand being in Reverend Engle's school. He

sometimes daydreamed, wriggled in his seat, or kicked the chair in front of him. Each time he did, Reverend Engle was sure to catch him. One reason Al had trouble learning in school may have been his poor hearing. Not being able to hear the teacher clearly could have made Al more restless and distracted.

After about three months, Al ran home from school and refused to go back. His mother wanted to know why. He told her he heard the teacher call him "addled," or confused. He told her how horrible each day had been, and how scared he was every minute he spent in that school. Mrs. Edison was furious. She brought Al back to the school and told Reverend Engle he didn't know what he was talking about. That was no way to run a school! She had been a teacher herself. She knew that children didn't learn by

being beaten and frightened.

"You are not going back to that place," Nancy Edison told her son. "I'll make up lessons for you at home. This will be your school, and I will be your teacher. I promise you'll learn more—and a lot faster—my way."

Edison said later, "My mother came out as my strong defender. . . . In fact, she was the most enthusiastic champion a boy ever had, and I determined right then that I would be worthy of her and show her that her confidence was not misplaced."

Al was much happier learning at home. Mrs. Edison had a simple way of teaching. She gave Al books to read. Then they talked about what he had read. By the time he was nine years old, Al had read *The Penny Encyclopedia*, Sears's *History of the World*, and many other books of history and fiction. He studied *Parker's School Com-*

pendium of *Natural* and *Experimental Philosophy*, which explained all that was known of science at the time, and he performed every experiment in it. He learned about astronomy, electricity, magnetism, light, and sound.

Al was a very fast reader. He enjoyed his mother's praise for finishing each book so quickly. He also earned another reward. Mr. Edison paid Al a quarter for each book the boy read and understood.

Mrs. Edison's belief in him was important to young Al. "My mother was always kind, always sympathetic, and she never misunderstood or misjudged me," he said. "If it had not been for her appreciation and her faith in me at a critical time in my experience, I should very likely never have become an inventor."

Al's mother also gave him lessons in arithmetic, geography, and penmanship.

He was a fine pupil when it came to geography and penmanship. He had good, clear handwriting, and he could draw very nicely. The maps he made were as neat and well done as any printed map in a book.

But when it came to arithmetic, Al struggled. For the rest of his life, arithmetic remained a puzzle to Edison. When he became an inventor, and the plans for one of his experiments needed math to be done, he asked one of his assistants to do it. Edison could imagine new and wonderful inventions. He could draw plans for the things he imagined. He could name and describe each part. But he often turned to others when the plans needed work with numbers.

CHAPTER 4:
A Great Success

Al's father also helped with the boy's education. Mr. Edison was in charge of a lighthouse at the edge of Lake Huron. Part of his job was to take care of the boiler and the fog whistle. Whenever Mr. Edison had to oil or repair the engine, he brought Al along.

The boy loved to help his father work on the two-horsepower engine. It had a large, turning cogwheel and a lever that opened a valve to let steam through the whistle. The force of the steam made the whistle blow.

Al never tired of watching how the cog-wheel worked. He must have learned a lot because the cogwheel played an important part in many of his early inventions.

Al also learned how to run a business. When he was eleven years old, he and Michael Oates, a boy who did chores for the Edisons, sold vegetables. They gathered onions, cabbage, lettuce, peas, turnips, beets, potatoes, and carrots and loaded them all on an open wagon. Then they hitched a horse to the wagon and peddled the vegetables in nearby towns.

Al's business was a huge success. People liked to buy vegetables from the farm, delivered right to their doors. On most days, he brought the wagon home

empty. When his customers asked him if he had any fresh fruit, Al had another idea. He went to farmers who had fruit for sale. He bought their apples, pears, peaches, and plums and sold them at a good profit.

The boys did very well at their work. After Al paid his partner, he made a profit of over six hundred dollars! That was a lot of money in 1858. In those days, food cost much less than it does now.

The Edisons were proud of their son's hard work and good business sense. Many grown-ups didn't make so much money in a whole year! Al had paid for all the food he carried on the wagon, he had paid Michael for helping him, and he still came away with more than six hundred dollars. What impressed his parents most was that Al turned over every penny of that money to them. It was, he said, for his share of the family expenses.

CHAPTER 5:
Al's Experiments

Al found time for other things besides business and reading. Every evening, after supper, he went down to the cellar. There he had set up a science laboratory. It wasn't much more than an old worktable, a few shelves, and some bottles and pans. But he had enough equipment to try all kinds of experiments.

Whenever Al had pocket money, he spent it on chemicals. Soon he had more than two hundred bottles filled with chemicals. When his mother insisted

he label the bottles, he marked each one POISON. Some of the chemicals weren't dangerous at all, but Al wanted to make sure that nobody touched anything in his laboratory. He knew what every bottle contained.

Al taught himself chemistry from books of experiments. He loved to mix liquids and powders and see what happened. He was really pleased when his experiments came out just the way a book said they would.

Sometimes Al had an idea that didn't come from a book. Once he decided to test a chemical called Seidlitz powder. The powder fizzed when added to water, and people took it for stomachaches. Al watched the way bubbles rose when the chemical was mixed with water. It made him think of the way a balloon filled with gas rose into the air. He wondered what would happen if someone took a very large amount of Seidlitz powder mixed in water. Would that person lift up off the ground and fly away?

Al asked his business partner, Michael Oates, to try it. At first, he wasn't too keen on being the guinea pig. He wondered how he would get back down.

Al told him he could grab onto a branch of a tree above him. Then Al would climb up a ladder to bring him back down. "Science needs brave people," he told Michael, "people who aren't afraid to try something new. You're not afraid, are you?"

"I'm not afraid," Michael said. "But are you sure it's safe?"

"Of course," Al answered. "Every one of my experiments has worked. This one will, too. Anyway, don't you want to be the first human being to fly?"

Michael liked that idea. "All right, he said. "Let's do it."

Al mixed a large dose of Seidlitz powder and water. It fizzed and bubbled, and Michael drank every drop. Then the boys went outside and waited for Michael to lift off the ground. For a while, nothing happened. Then Michael started to groan with pain. He had a terrible stomachache.

Michael's loud groans brought Mr. and Mrs. Edison running out of the house. They soon learned the cause of Michael's pain. "You were foolish to swallow chemicals you know nothing about," Mr. Edison told Michael sternly. "That stomachache should teach you a lesson. I don't think you'll do anything like that again. As for you, Al, I'm going to teach you a lesson!"

Mr. Edison's lesson was a sound spanking. Mrs. Edison told the young scientist to clear his junk out of the cellar. Al begged for another chance. He swore he'd never do another experiment on people, he'd keep his laboratory locked, and he'd stick to experiments that came out of books. Al's parents gave it a lot of thought, and finally they agreed.

CHAPTER 6:
Working Hard

In 1859, right after he turned twelve, Al started working. In those days, many young people went to work. In the nineteenth century, most young people finished school and found jobs before they were teenagers. What was unusual was the way Al earned his money.

A train ran between Port Huron and Detroit, Michigan. The trip took three hours each way. Al was sure the passengers would get hungry and bored in that time. Why not sell them newspapers, books,

magazines, fruit, and candy? He asked railroad officials for permission to sell these
goods on the train. They said yes, and he
was in business.

Every morning, Al got up early and filled
two baskets with food, books, magazines,
and newspapers. He got on the train at Port
Huron at seven. For the next three hours,

he sold his goods up and down the aisles of the passenger cars.

When the train arrived in Detroit, Al stored his baskets in the baggage car. He got off the train, ate, and stocked up on supplies to sell on the way back. Then he hurried to the Detroit Public Library, where he sat and read for hours. "I didn't read a few books," he said. "I read the library."

Whenever Al had money to spare, he went to a drug supply company and bought

chemicals. He needed them for the new experiments he was reading about.

At half-past six each evening, he got back on the train for the trip home. Then he took his baskets out of the baggage car and went to work again. During the three-hour return trip to Port Huron, he walked up and down the cars, selling snacks and the Detroit afternoon newspapers.

Al didn't get home until ten o'clock at night. He ate a quick supper and crawled into bed. Every day was long and busy. Even so, he complained that he wasn't doing as much as he could. He wanted to try so many experiments, but Sunday was his only free day. So he put his brain to work and came up with a solution to his problem.

The baggage car on the train was never filled. Al got permission to set up a laboratory there. Before long, he was

spending part of each trip mixing powders and liquids, learning more and more
with each new experiment.

CHAPTER 7:
Al the Inventor

Al had his experiments to do and his business to run, but even that wasn't enough for a boy with such endless energy. When he was thirteen, Al opened two stores in Port Huron. One sold newspapers and magazines. The other sold fruits, vegetables, and dairy products Al bought from farmers along the railroad line. Al supplied both stores with stock and hired a boy to run each store. He also hired boys to sell bread, newspapers, and candy on other daily trains.

All of that still wasn't enough for Al.
Every moment he didn't use for something worthwhile was wasted, as far as he
was concerned. Years later, when Edison
became famous, people marveled at how
hard he worked, how little he slept, and

how many useful things he invented. Not many of them knew he had set the pattern back in the days when he worked on the Port Huron–Detroit train.

Often, when he was asked the secret of his success, the great inventor repeated his two favorite mottoes: "Genius is one percent inspiration and ninety-nine percent perspiration" and "There is no substitute for hard work."

One day, Al was running to catch a train. A man on the train grabbed him by the ears and pulled him up. Al felt something crack in both ears. From then on, his hearing kept getting worse.

In 1860, telephones had not yet been invented. That summer, Al became interested in telegraphy, a method of sending messages through wires using electrical signals. Al read every book he could find on telegraphy. Then he and a friend set up a telegraph line between their houses. They strung stovepipe wire from tree to tree. Late at night, they sent messages back and forth. They became faster and faster at tapping out their messages—until a cow got tangled in the line and wrecked it.

CHAPTER 8:
Wartime

The next year, in April of 1861, the Civil War began. Al found that newspaper sales on his train route were booming. People could not wait for word about the latest battles, lists of wounded soldiers, and the news from President Lincoln's office. This change gave Al another idea—to print his own newspaper. Called *The Weekly Herald*, it was printed by Al in the same baggage car of the Port Huron–Detroit train where his lab was set up.

The Weekly Herald reported local news from the towns along the railroad line. It also ran news of the war, which Al got from telegraphers at stops along the line. Pretty soon, the paper was making a fine profit. Al earned money to spend on chemicals and books.

Unfortunately, one day, the train lurched, and one of his chemicals fell. It started a fire in the baggage car. The conductor helped him put out the fire, but he was so angry he threw Al, his lab equipment, and his printing press out at the next station. The press and much of the lab equipment were ruined. From then on, Al had to sell newspapers at train stations.

In August 1862, Al was waiting in the Mount Clemens train station. He saw a small child playing on the railroad tracks. A moment later, Al was horrified to see a freight car coming. He threw down his bundle of papers, ran, and pulled the child to safety.

The child's father, James Mackenzie, was the Mount Clemens station telegraph operator. He was so grateful that he offered to teach Al how to become a telegraph operator. For three months, they worked together four days a week. "By this time," Mr. Mackenzie remembered, "he knew as much about telegraphy as I did."

Because it was wartime, the Union Army needed experienced telegraphers. Many men answered the call. Civilian jobs opened up for beginners like Al. At sixteen, he found work at the Port Huron telegraph office. His salary was $25 a month.

For the next few years, Al Edison worked as a telegraph operator in cities and towns

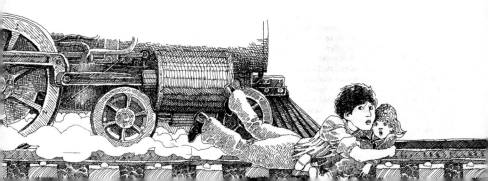

all over the United States and Canada. He was known for his clear handwriting, and he became one of the fastest operators who worked for Western Union. He also got into trouble for sleeping on the job. He was tired from staying awake to work on his experiments.

During those years as a telegrapher, Edison began inventing things. He built a mechanical vote recorder, but it was not popular. After that, he decided he would only work on inventions people would use. He designed improvements to a stock ticker, a machine that took stock prices from a telegraph wire and printed them on a strip of paper. That work earned him $40,000, a huge amount in those days. The money allowed him to become a full-time inventor.

CHAPTER 9:
A Great Genius

Thomas Alva Edison created hundreds of inventions that changed the way the world lived. They include the electric lightbulb and the phonograph, an early record player. Every time Edison invented something, he recorded his creation with the U.S. Patent Office. Holding a patent on the invention meant that Edison was recognized as the inventor. It also meant that he was the only one who could produce the invention or profit from it. The U.S. Patent Office granted Edison a total of 1,093

patents, more than any other person ever received. Among these were important inventions dealing with motion pictures, the telephone, the telegraph, cement making, electric railroads, the storage battery, and electric power plants.

In 1871, Edison married Mary Stillwell. Together, they had three children, Marion, Thomas Alva Jr., and William. Mary died in 1884, and two years later, Edison remarried. With his second wife, Mina Miller, he had three more children, Madeleine, Charles, and Theodore.

Thomas Alva Edison devoted all of his adult life to science. As he grew older, Edison's hearing grew worse and worse, until he became almost totally deaf. He said many times that his hearing loss helped him concentrate on his work. Several of his inventions were intended to help people hear better.

Once he had made enough money to be free from worry, he built a huge laboratory in Menlo Park, New Jersey. He hired a team of scientists and gave them everything they needed to work. Their only job was to dream up new inventions.

This idea—paying scientists just to think up experiments and try them out—had never been tried before. Edison's team was so successful that others copied his brilliant idea of scientific "dreamwork." Today, many large companies and universities have research departments. The whole idea began with Edison's group in Menlo Park.

October 21, 1929, was the fiftieth anniversary of Edison's invention of the electric light. Two years later, after his death on October 18, 1931, these words were spoken at his funeral: "Picture an electric lightless, an electric powerless, a telephoneless, a motion pictureless, a phonographless world, and a faint realization of his greatness dawns upon us. By taking Edison and his works out of the world, we gain the keenest appreciation of Edison in the world."

These words are a fitting tribute to Thomas Alva Edison's unique genius.

INDEX